Materials, Materials, Materials

Soil

Chris Oxlade

Heinemann Library
Chicago, Illinois

© 2002 Reed Educational & Professional Publishing
Published by Heinemann Library,
an imprint of Reed Educational & Professional Publishing,
Chicago, Illinois

Customer Service 888-454-2279

Visit our website at www.heinemannlibrary.com

Designed by Storeybooks
Originated by Ambassador Litho
Printed and bound in Hong Kong/China

06 05 04 03 02
10 9 8 7 6 5 4 3 2 1

Library of Congress Cataloging-in-Publication Data
Oxlade, Chris.
  Soil / Chris Oxlade.
      p. cm. -- (Materials, materials, materials)
Includes bibliographical references (p.   ).
Summary: A simple presentation of information about soil, including its
composition, properties, and some of its uses.
  ISBN 1-58810-587-3 (lib. bdg.)   ISBN 1-4034-0088-1 (pbk. bdg.)
  1. Soils--Juvenile literature. 2. Soil biology--Juvenile literature.
[1. Soils.] I. Title. II. Series.
  S591.3 .O84 2001
  631.4--dc21
                                 2001003928

Acknowledgments
The author and publishers are grateful to the following for permission to reproduce copyright materi-
al: p. 4 Sally Morgan/Ecoscene; p. 5 Chinch Gryniewicz/Ecoscene; pp. 6, 7, 19 Tudor Photography; p. 8
FLPA; pp. 9, 15 Andrew Brown/Ecoscene; p. 10 Corbis; p. 11 Zul Mukhida/Chapel Studios; pp. 12, 14, 18,
26 GSF Picture Library; pp. 13, 22 Still Pictures; p. 16 David M. Dennis/Oxford Scientific Films; p. 17
Science Photo Library; p. 20 Piers Cavendish/Impact; p. 21 Irvine Cushing/Oxford Scientific Films; p. 23
Tony Page/Ecoscene; p. 24 Hodder Wayland; p. 25 Ecoscene; p. 27 Oxford Scientific Films; p. 29 Eric
Soder/NHPA.

Cover photograph reproduced with permission of Image Bank.

Some words are shown in bold, **like this.** You can find out what
they mean by looking in the glossary.

Contents

What Is Soil?

Soil is a **natural** material. Soil covers the top of the ground in gardens, fields, meadows, and many other places. Plants grow in soil.

4

Plants cannot live without soil, from tiny flowers to huge trees. Soil contains **nutrients** and water that plants need to grow.

What Is in Soil?

Soil is made of different materials. One material is rock that has been broken into small pieces. Some bits of rock are large pebbles. Others are tiny grains.

Soil also contains bits of dead plants, such as leaves and twigs. They slowly **rot** away. These rotten bits are called **humus.** Humus contains **nutrients** that keep soil healthy.

Soil Colors

There are many different kinds of soil. This soil contains tiny grains of rock that make it a browny-red color. It is called clay.

8

This soil is dark brown. It contains many **rotting** roots and leaves. It is called peat. It is found in wet, **marshy** places.

9

Soil and Water

There are small spaces of air between the bits that make up soil. In sandy soil, the spaces between the grains of sand are big. This way, rainwater can quickly **drain** away.

The bits of rock in clay soil are very tiny. There are only small spaces between the bits. Rainwater cannot drain through them quickly. It lies on top of the clay in puddles.

Rocks in the Soil

The bits of rock in soil come from big rocks and mountains. Over time, they are broken up by wind and water.

12

When rain falls on the ground, it
washes the bits of rock into streams
and rivers. If the river floods, the
rocky soil is left on the land next
to the river.

13

Humus

Humus is the name for the bits of dead plants in the soil. Humus is made of leaves that fall from trees and parts of dead plants.

14

The leaves and dead plants slowly **rot** away. They turn brown and mushy. After a while, they become part of the soil. Humus helps keep the soil from drying up.

Animals in the Soil

Many different animals live in the soil. Worms **burrow** through the soil. As they burrow, they break up the soil. This lets air and water into it and helps plants grow.

Millions of tiny creatures live in the soil. They are so small you can only see them with a **microscope.** This picture shows what some of them look like through a microscope.

Growing in Soil

As a plant grows, its roots grow down into the soil. Roots grip the soil and keep plants from blowing over in the wind.

The roots of a plant soak up water and **nutrients** from the soil. Tiny root hairs stick out from the root. They collect the water and nutrients.

Growing Crops

Farmers grow **crops** in fields of soil. Before they plant seeds, they have to get the soil ready. They dig it over with a **plow.** This brings fresh soil to the top.

Gardeners also prepare soil before they plant seeds. They dig up the soil with a tool called a spade. This brings fresh soil to the top and breaks it into small pieces.

Keeping Soil Fresh

Plants take **nutrients** from the soil. When plants die, they **rot** away. This puts the nutrients back into the soil. Gardeners add rotted plants to the soil to keep it healthy.

22

Farmers gather up all the **crops** in their fields. This means there are no plants left to put nutrients into the soil. The farmer has to add **fertilizer** to put the nutrients back.

Building with Soil

Soil can be used to build strong walls called banks. Banks keep the water inside a river after it rises from a heavy rainfall.

24

Farmers grow rice in fields called rice paddies. Rice needs a lot of water to grow. The farmers build banks of soil around the fields to keep the water in.

Spoiling Soil

Soil washes away easily. If too many trees are cut down, there are no tree roots to hold the soil together. Then, heavy rain can wash the soil away.

Soil can be spoiled by **pollution.** When
garbage and **chemicals** are spilled onto
the soil it is hard for plants to grow. Only
some strong weeds can survive.

Fact File

- Soil is a **natural** material.

- Soil comes in different colors.

- All soil has tiny pieces of rock in it.

- Some soil has large pieces of rock in it.

- Some soil lets water **drain** away easily.

- Some soil does not let water drain away.

- Soil contains **nutrients** that plants need to live and grow.

- Soil does not burn when it is heated.

- Soil does not let **electricity** flow through it.

- Soil is not attracted by **magnets.**

28

Can You Believe It?

Earthworms eat soil as they **burrow** through it! They take the nutrients out of the soil and pass the rest out again. A worm cast is a tiny heap of soil that a worm has eaten.

Glossary

burrow when an animal digs a hole as it moves around underground

chemical material used to clean or protect something

crop plant that farmers grow for food, such as wheat or potatoes

drain when water or another liquid moves through and away from a material

electricity form of power that can light lamps, heat houses, and make things work

factory big building where things are made using machines

fertilizer spray or powder that helps plants grow

humus part of soil that is made from bits of dead plants

magnet piece of iron or steel that pulls iron or steel things toward it

marsh area of land that is very wet

microscope machine that makes things look bigger than they are

natural comes from plants, animals, or rocks in the earth

nutrient food that plants or people need to grow and be healthy

plow machine that breaks up soil to make it ready for planting seeds

pollution harmful chemicals in the air, rivers, and seas

rot to fall apart over time because of dampness

More Books to Read

Bailey, Jill. *Worm*. Chicago: Heinemann Library, 1998.

Bockneck, Jonathan. *The Science of Soil*. Milwaukee: Gareth Stevens, 1999.

Flanagan, Alice. *Soil*. Minneapolis: Compass Point Books, 2000.

Madgwick, Wendy. *Super Materials*. Austin, Tex.: Raintree Steck-Vaughn, 1999.

Index